Author profile http://www.ebooksbydarren.com

Blog http://www.darrenackers.com/

Twitter https://twitter.com/darren_ackers

LinkedIn https://uk.linkedin.com/in/darrenackers

I0503452

Table of Contents

Disclaimer and FTC Compliance

No part of this book may be reproduced, or stored in a retrieval system, or transmitted in any form or by any means, electronic, mechanical, photocopying, recording, or otherwise without express written permission of the author.

This book is for the sole purpose of entertainment. All the views detailed in this book are those of the author, therefore should not be taken as any form of instruction of an expert. The reader is solely responsible for their actions.

Both the author and the publisher does not accept any responsibility or liability whatsoever on behalf of the purchaser or reader of these materials.

As an affiliate marketer my eBooks on occasions contain affiliate links - simply put, I will receive a commission payment on a purchase through the affiliate link. I advise you to carry out your own research before completing a purchase. All affiliate products I promote in my eBooks are products that I have personally used and have found to be useful.

Strategic Thinking Before You Begin

Before you begin and dive into social media marketing, you must devise a clear strategy. The most important part of your strategy is to define which age generation you plan to target. Here's a breakdown of today's generations:

Generation	Born
Baby Boomers	1946-1964
Generation X	1964-1980
Generation Y or Millennials	1980-2000
Generation Z	2000 – present day

You need to carry extensive research and decide which social platform your target generation(s) is using and the type of message to use. For example, the image below shows the average teenager hangs out on social media. The Pew Research Center, a Washington, D.C 'Fact Tank' found that 71% of teens use Facebook which makes Facebook the most popular social platform among US teens. So if you are marketing to teens, it makes perfect sense to focus more of your efforts on Facebook and Instagram and less on Tumblr.

How to Market Your Product or Service the Simple Way

Marketing your business or product online can be a minefield, let's face it, with the many, many social media sites and applications that exist, you can easily spread yourself too thin. The key to online marketing is to initially select a few online marketing methods and to track and monitor the desired results they generate.

You might have the greatest product, a service that solves problems and produces an awesome ROI for your customer. Without a solid online marketing strategy you could be on the road to failure. The good news is there are plenty of ways to successfully market your business or product using both free and paid marketing methods. By creating and implementing a well thought out marketing plan, you will succeed, providing you align your message to your potential customers' requirements. Obviously you do not want to promise or deliver a message which is so far from the truth; your message needs to be exactly what your potential customers expect.

In this book, I have put together an extensive range of marketing techniques for businesses to market themselves using tested online methods – whether it be Social Media, Email Marketing or Social Selling. I have been involved in Sales & Marketing B2B and B2C for over eighteen years. Over the past few years I have tested various online marketing methods. You will discover what I've learnt and I will share with you a list of ways which I have found to be successful to market a business or product online.

You may already have implemented some of my marketing methods, but I do hope that you will learn some new marketing techniques. To make this book easy to follow, I've tried to write in a get to the point style with detail instructions on how to use certain online applications and sites. Before you get stuck in to my book, I want to begin by briefly discussing social media etiquette, since this is a vital 'common sense' approach which many social media users get wrong.

Social Media Etiquette

It astonishes me how many LinkedIn and Twitter users are not respectful and do not consider the way they communicate with other social media users. Building relationships online is exactly the same as building relationships offline. To build any relationship you need to treat others the same as you like to be treated. The biggest mistake I see on social media is how eager an individual is to pitch a new connection, immediately after connecting with them.

If you were at a party and a stranger came up to you, introduced themselves, and then immediately started pitching to you, my guess is you would think this person is an idiot and at the first chance move as far away from them as possible. The same goes for networking, online or offline. With a new connection, always remember you need to earn the right to pitch to them. Before pitching them, you must earn their trust, engage with them, and build a relationship with them. The best way to engage with a social media connection is to share useful content, send them content which solves a challenge they have, like their updates, comment on their updates, wish them happy birthday, send them invitations, and basically be 'human'.

Google Chrome Browser – The Social Enthusiast Web Browser

For the past few years I have chosen to use the Chrome browser by Google. What I like about this browser is the ability to add apps and extensions and cloud functionality to sync across iPad, iPhone and my PC. Just like Apple's App Store, you can download a plethora of applications and extensions which are both free and paid for. The difference between an app and extension is that an extension is added to the right of the search bar. Extensions typically require you to download them, whereas an app is more like browsing websites, by this I mean you don't normally need to download them.

Here's a list of my favorite Google Chrome apps and extensions.

Dropbox

Dropbox allows you to store photos and documents in the cloud and then sync your stored documents and photos with your PC, Tablet or Cellphone. I recommend upgrading to Dropbox Pro because for $99 per year you will receive 1,000 GB of space: 1,000 GB of space roughly stores 2 million photos or 250,000 songs.

Evernote

Evernote is a cloud based extension and is used to store and create notes. Again it can be synced across multiple devices. I use the free version of Evernote and regularly create new notes and add to existing notes. When I'm researching topics to write about, I create a note and then keep adding ideas which pop into my head. Another way I use Evernote is to capture anything I come across on the web which will help me become better in my day job. For example, I read a lot of sales and marketing articles, so when I come across useful information, I simply cut and paste into an Evernote note. I also use Evernote to track my gym and fitness programmes.

Buffer

I love Buffer because it allows me to share and schedule content (articles) across all my favorite social platforms at a click of a button. Buffer is available as either free or paid for versions. I use the free version which satisfies my needs nicely. Buffer also provides insights on how visible and engaged your shared content was – to see these insights, click on 'Analytics' tab.

Riffle

Riffle by CrowdRiff is a Twitter dashboard allowing you to perform analytics and insights on Twitter. For example, I use Riffle to spy on a Twitter user to gather intelligence before reaching out to them. By searching on their Twitter user name you can see their top used hashtags, top mentions, number of tweets, their followers and who they follow. Furthermore, you can find out their Klout Score. A Klout Score is a number between 1-100 – this represents how active you are on social media. The higher the number (supposedly) means you're more influential. For example, Barack Obama and Justin Bieber have Klout Scores above 90.

Pocket

Pocket is an extension and is great way to save articles, videos, images etc found on the web. Once you found something of interest, you can click the Pocket icon and read it later. Pocket syncs across your tablet, PC and cellphone – this makes what you saved readily available on all your devices.

Pocket works nicely with IFTT – an abbreviation of 'If This Then That'. IFTTT is a web service that allows users to create simple commands called 'Recipes' – these are automatic triggers based on changes it finds on the web. A great social recipe is to send an automatic tweet thanking your new follower. If you do use this 'Auto thank new Twitter followers' recipe, be sure to add a couple of hashtags to your message and of course, DO NOT make your message salesy or promotional. I discuss IFTTT in a later chapter.

Dux-Soup LinkedIn Automation

Dux-Soup is a browser add-on plugin for Google Chrome. It's available as a free version or paid Pro version. The way it works is by keeping track of the users you view on LinkedIn and allows you to make notes in a box about the LinkedIn user you are viewing. In addition, the Pro version allows you to auto visit LinkedIn profiles based on searches you make on Google or on LinkedIn. Viewing LinkedIn profiles is a great tool for business development because the users you visit will most likely look at your profile or ask you to connect with them.

Content Curating and Curation

Posting and sharing content across social platforms are the foundation and building blocks for anyone who wants to excel at social media. The easiest method is 'content curation' – this is when you share content which is not your own. For example, you might read a great article related to your niche and want to share it on LinkedIn and Twitter.

When sharing content you should focus on sharing content related to your target market or industry and always share interesting content and nothing boring! Because I work in sales and marketing, I find that sharing 2 or 3 articles per day on LinkedIn is about right. Only sharing 2 or 3 articles per day shouldn't make you come across as a spammer and make your contact 'unfollow' you. Then every sixth share, I share semi promotional content about my company or products I sell. These semi promotional shares could be customer reviews, details of a new product, good news about your company etc.

The idea behind sharing content related to your industry is for you to been seen as a 'thought leader' – someone who is knowledgeable about something specific within their niche or industry. In a perfect world we would have a marketing department pump out content for us to share. In the real world this doesn't happen since generally marketing struggles to generate enough content for the sales department. Another great tip is to share popular content, for example, top articles on LinkedIn in your sector published by an

Influencer. I always try to add an image when sharing content because it is proven articles with images are read more.

How to Find Content

Finding great content to share is relatively easy when you know where to look. Here's a few ways to get you started: LinkedIn Pulse, Google Alerts, Industry Associations, Industry Bodies, RSS Feeds, Ask Suppliers, Ask Work Colleagues, Forbes, Inc, Entrepreneur, LinkedIn Influencers and Paper.li.

LinkedIn Pulse

Pulse owned by LinkedIn is an app which aggregates news and articles on a plethora of topics using RSS feeds. RSS feeds named 'Really Simple Syndication' are real-time feeds which publish news to an RSS Reader. An RSS Reader makes sense of the RSS code and displays the content so you can read it. Pulse can be accessed through the LinkedIn web site or through an OS or Android app. Pulse allows you to select topics of interest and then each day, fresh and new content will be sitting there ready for you to share.

Google Alerts

Google Alerts is a free monitoring service by Google which monitors the web for interesting and current content and news. Simply set up an alert and Google will forward you a daily email each time it finds matching content related to your alert. What I love about Google Alerts is that it can used to monitor your competition or companies you're looking to target and give you interesting insights.

Websites

I'm always looking for new websites and blogs to bookmark and sign up to for content. Websites which I use for content sharing are

Forbes, Entrepreneur, Hubspot, LinkedIn and Inc. When sharing LinkedIn Pulse content I always aim to share popular content preferably by a LinkedIn Influencer.

Paper.li

Paper.li is a free online newspaper which provides a platform to access a universe of articles, blog posts and web content. You have complete control of the content which it aggregates and displays on your personalized Paper.li newspaper. Furthermore, you have the option to automatically share the content each day to Twitter, Facebook, Google+ and LinkedIn.

Buffer

We previously discussed Buffer, but now I want to tell you more about this awesome online application. There are many applications online used to share content across social media profiles, for example: Buffer, AddThis, Hootsuite and Klout. By far, my favorite is Buffer because it's easy to use and uses a simple user interface. I use the free version of Buffer, but there is a paid version called Awesome. For the average social media user, the free Buffer is more than adequate. Once again, Buffer is a tool used to share and schedule content across multiple social media platforms. Buffer also connects with IFTTT (previously mentioned) and has its own IFTTT Recipe. A IFTTT Recipe which I use all the time is the one which connects Pocket with Buffer. By using this Recipe, you can favorite a piece of content when using Google Chrome via the Pocket app and this piece of content will be scheduled and shared through Buffer.

I have the Buffer app installed to my Google Chrome browser, so when I come across great content I simply click the Buffer app and schedule this content. In addition, I use the Buffer app on my iPad and iPhone. To use the Buffer app like I do, you first need to set it up on your iPhone. To set this up you need to tap the 'Share' button on your iPhone and scroll to the right and tap more. The next screen displays the 'Share Sheet'; the 'share sheet' lets you select which apps you would like to use on the Share button, so you would select 'Buffer'. You can also rearrange the apps on the 'Share Sheet' by holding your finger down and dragging them around.

IFTTT

IFTTT stands for 'If This Then That'. Like Buffer, it's available through a browser or via an android or OS app. IFTTT works by creating 'Recipes' - these are powerful statements to connect a plethora of online services and apps. There are various recipes to source content. Whilst we are discussing IFTTT, here's an example of a cool Twitter Recipe: 'Build a Twitter List from a specific #hashtag'. This recipe works by crawling Twitter for certain #hashtags and then placing the Twitter user tweeting with this #hashtag in a Twitter List. I shall discuss 'Twitter Lists' in a later chapter.

DrumUp and Scoop.it

These are two popular social tools to source relevant content for your social sharing efforts. I prefer DrumUp because DrumUp displays new articles, less than a week old, after you tell it which keywords you are interested in. It will also schedule articles that you want shared with your followers, this is a handy feature which is similar to what Buffer offers.

Klout

Klout has two uses: one is the Klout Score, and the other is the ability to source and share content. I know firsthand that the Klout Score is extremely important to some social media enthusiasts. The score is a grade between 1 and 100. The higher the number, (supposedly) you are better at social media.

The Klout Score is determined by the size of the users social media network and measures the content shared and how the user engages with their network. According to Wikipedia, some employers make hiring decisions based on Klout Scores. Klout is available through a web browser and IOS/ Android apps. What I do like about Klout is the ability to perform social media analytics. The analytics will show you how your Klout Score has performed during a 90 day periodand at a glance you can see how well you have engaged across various social media platforms.

Building an Image Library

If you're serious about sharing across social media platforms, I strongly advise you to build an online image library. By having an image library to hand, you can easily add images and photos to you content sharing. By adding an image to a share will at least double the chances of your content being read and shared by followers. There's two popular free image design services for social media, they are: Pablo by Buffer and Canva, owned by Guy Kawasaki. I recommend both services, but my favorite is Canva. Canva is very simple to use and has hundreds of images available to use. They also offer a premium library where images only cost $1. Canva is the perfect solution to create blog graphics, presentations, Twitter covers, YouTube covers, flyers, posters and so much more. You can also upload your own images and photos for editing.

Storing Your Images

Once you have your images created, I recommend you store them in one place. For example, you can store images using any of the following: Dropbox, Flickr, Facebook Page, Instagram and Pinterest. Remember you can easily share an image stored on any of the above websites by installing the 'Add This' extension to Google Chrome browser. Once installed, all you need to do is tap the Add This icon and voila – your image is stored. Furthermore, Buffer will also allow you to share an image on a webpage.

Add This

Like I said, Add This is available as a Google Chrome extension, once installed the icon will sit on the top right of the screen next to the search bar. Add This connects to over 300 social media platforms and allows you to customize the selection so your favorite social media platforms appear in order of preference. Another plus to using Add This is it doesn't slow your browser speed. Add This share buttons can also be installed on your own website or blog. If you have a Word Press blog, I prefer to use a social sharing plugin such as WP Social Sharing by Arjun Jain. The reason I like this plugin is the fact it installs social sharing buttons at the top or bottom of each blog post and includes your Twitter handle when someone shares your post on Twitter within your blog post.

Include Your Twitter Handle

Too many blogs use social sharing buttons which do not allow the blog owner to include their Twitter handle when someone tweets within their blog. You read a great blog post and decide to share this fruitful post to your Twitter followers. You hit the Twitter share button and your followers get to read this great article. But wait, where and what is the blog author's Twitter handle. When I share useful articles on Twitter, I always give credit to the author of the article. If you are not using a social sharing Wordpress plugin which allows you to include your Twitter handle, well you are missing out big time!

Word Swag

I would like to introduce you to a very cool design app which I use on my iPhone and iPad. Word Swag is a low cost design app where you can create attractive custom test layouts that would normally take hours to create, but with this app, designing custom text on images takes seconds. The way I use Word Swag is to add text to my stored images and photos and then share the final image across my social media platforms.

Why Social Listening Is so Important

Social listening should be an important part to your social media tool kit. Social listening is a way to track and monitor what is said on the web about you and others. You can use social listening to monitor what's said about you, your competition or prospects. I mainly use social listening to monitor what my connections, clients and prospective clients are up to. Here are a few free tools to perform social listening:

Google Alerts
Google Alerts is an automated way to discover what is being said on the web. Sign up using your Google account and simply enter keywords and phrases to monitor. Google will then email you data related to your keywords and phrases. Google Alerts is great for sourcing content, spying on competition and listening to what is being said about you on the web.

Social Mention
Social Mention is another free online tool used to listen and monitor across over one hundred social media sites. Social Mention does a good job of summarizing what it finds as Strength, Passion, Sentiment and Reach.

Hootsuite
Hootsuite is similar to Buffer in that it can be used to share content. Hootsuite offers more functionality than Buffer and is a useful social listening tool. Hootsuite has free and paid versions; my advice is start with the free version before upgrading to the paid one.

Hootsuite at first glance has a technical interface, but once you take the time to learn Hootsuite, you will see it's easy to navigate. You can also sign up for free training by a Hootsuite trainer.

Newsle

Newsle was acquired by LinkedIn and is an awesome tool to monitor your LinkedIn connections. Newsle works by scanning the web in real-time and notifies you when one of your LinkedIn connections publishes an article, blog post or is featured in the news. The notification happens in seconds who allows you to get in touch with your connection and build a deeper relationship with them. Newsle doesn't pick up any social noise such as Tweets and Facebook updates. What it does is present the real news about your connection. My advice is always to reach out to your connection as soon as possible if you are going to congratulate them in some way.

A Quick Word on Wordpress

If you don't have a WordPress blog, then you need to get one fast. WordPress is a free open source application that allows you to build simple but very attractive websites. Once you install WordPress on a domain name, you can then customize your WordPress application in a variety of ways and creative plug-ins.

Many well known brands and websites use Wordpress as a platform to build their website. Here are a few examples:

The Wall Street Journal Blogs
Time Magazine Blogs
CNN Blogs
TED Blog
People Magazine StyleNews
Wired Blogs
Forbes Blogs
Yahoo News India
CBS New York
The New York Observer
Harvard University Gazette
Reader's Digest
MTV Newsroom

If you have read any of my books, you will know how much I rate Wordpress to create a website. The Wordpress I'm talking about here is the one you host or is hosted by a hosting company such as Bluehost. To be clearer, I mean when you register your own domain name, for example, darrenackers.com and not wordpress.darrenackers.com. In my opinion, you should never take the shortcut and create a Wordpress site which is not on a domain name you own. If we take the example wordpress.darrenackers.com, I do not own this domain and Wordpress.com does. There are two things wrong with hosting a blog on a Wordpres.com type domain, they are: One, you have limited functionality versus a blog published on a domain you own. Two, at anytime a site on Wordpress.com could be taken down because you do not own your site – Wordpress.com owns your site because it's on their domain name.

One issue to look out for with Wordpress is that pages tend to load slowly. I'm by no way an SEO guru, but I do know that your site needs to load pretty fast to achieve high organic search results on Google. Furthermore, visitors to your site are more likely to stay on it longer when pages on a site load fast. With this in mind, you need to install a plugin to speed up the time a page takes to load such as W3 Total Cache. The plugin developers claim their W3 Total Cache can improve a Wordpress sites performance by up to 10 times.

You should also have a SEO plugin installed so you can change the pages title, description and META keywords – all this is essential for search engines to index and read your site. As standard, Wordpress installations do not allow you to customize the pages title, description and META keywords. Furthermore, an SEO plugin will generate XML sitemaps which again are essential for search engines to rank your site in their organic results. I use the All in One SEO Pack plugin to help automatically optimize my Wordpress sites.

Another of my favorite plugins is P3 by GoDaddy. This plugin monitors all the plugins installed on a Wordpress site and then reports on which plugins are making your Wordpress site slow to load.

I use Bluehost to host all my WordPress sites since they charge a very low annual fee to host an unlimited number of websites. They also provide excellent 24/7 technical support. There are many hosting companies like Bluehost that offer WordPress. If you do choose one of these hosting providers, you must insure they offer cPanel. cPanel is an easy-to-use dashboard to manage websites, email, domain names and much more. Click here to visit www.bluehost.com.

Even if you are based outside of the US, I strongly suggest you use a US based web hosting company. Why, because they offer cheaper rates and most use the cPanel. The problem with UK web hosting companies is that they typically charge per website to host, in the US you pay one fee and can host as many sites as you want.

Plus I think US technology companies tend to be more advanced than the UK, therefore you receive more value for your money regarding technology. The cPanel is awesome, it's incredibly user friendly and simple to navigate.

There are many tutorials on using WordPress. My advice is to learn WordPress since it is one of the most important tools to base your online marketing strategy on. My site is built on the WordPress platform.

YouTube Tips

YouTube is an awesome social media website which Google bought in October 2006 for a staggering 1.65 billion dollars. The site receives over 100 million views per day, so you can see it's a great free marketing tool.

Once you set up your channel on YouTube, you can then embed your videos on your website or blog. Better still, record a 20-minute video, make it private, and offer all your future customers this as a gift using email marketing.

Later in this book, I will discuss email list building using Aweber where you can offer subscribers a free gift. To record this private video, you can then use it to get future readers on your list. If you are familiar with affiliate marketing, you will understand exactly what I mean.

To record screen capture videos I use www.screencast-o-matic.com. I have used both Jing and Camtasia, but to be honest, I prefer www.screencast-o-matic.com since it's user friendly and is hosted online.

Here's how to record a YouTube video using Screencast.

Go to http://www.screencast-o-matic.com and register for a free account. To begin with I would just use the free version and then when you start to make money pay $15 for the annual pro version. The free version will give you -

- Max recording time of 15 minutes - this is more than enough recording time
- Free hosting for 15 videos that you record
- Record screen and webcam
- Publish your videos to YouTube at a click of the button

The paid version will let you record HD videos and allow you to access a variety of editing tools. I have the pro version but rarely use the editing tools. Why, because the videos are 4-5 minutes in length, and if I make a mistake I simply start again.

On their home page you will see the help section, just click on the button which is located at the top right. This will show you how to use the software to record videos.

Recording a video is straight forward; make sure you have a script prepared. Mistakes are easily made when recording videos and the most common are too many errs. Remember practice makes perfect. It may take you 4 or 5 takes before the video is ready to publish.

Remember to share your YouTube videos across all social platforms you use and embed them in your website.

Your Channel Art
YouTube allows you to upload a profile image to give your channel an identity which is called Channel Art. Here's Google's helpful link to find out more about channel art for your page https://support.google.com/youtube/answer/2972003?hl=en-GB.

You can also download a channel art template on this page which I encourage you to do.

When designing your own channel art, you must create the image so that it appears in the safe area which is the centre of the channel art image. The centre part of the image should measure 1546 x 423 px. The benefit by placing a 1546 x 423 px image in the centre is that your channel image will display correctly across all devices such as mobile, desktop, tablet and tv. I always download the channel art template from the above link and make the amendments in Paintshop Pro. An alternative is to head over to fiverr.com and purchase a gig to design you channel art for your YouTube page.

Chroma Key (Green Screen Tips)

A great way to create professional a video is to use Green Screen or commonly know Chroma Key. Chroma Key is a post-production editing technique when a green screen is used as the video background and then Chroma Key software is used to replace the green background with an image of your choice. Here are a few Chroma Key tips I've learnt:

1: Do not wear green when you shoot the video otherwise your green clothing could be replaced with the Chroma Key image when edited.

2: It's crucial your green screen is properly lit. The green screen needs to be lit evenly with no shadows by using lights either side and behind the green screen.

3: When using an iPhone or iPad on a tripod to record the video, you will also need a good quality microphone connected to your iPhone or iPad.

4: A green screen could be a large piece of fabric or wall painted green. Obviously the green you use must similar to the Chroma Key green color. Whatever you use, you must ensure the background is flat and even. If you use fabric you must pull the fabric tight and have no creases showing. Any crease could cause shadows which will darken the green and could ruin the video.

There are many free and paid for software applications available to edit green screen recordings. If you have a Mac, then iMovie does a good job editing green screen.

Annotations and End Slates

To get the most from your YouTube videos, you need to add annotations and end slates and of course a subscribe button. Annotations are used to enrich the video experience by adding information, links and other detail in boxes and speech bubbles. It is very simple to add annotations. To create an annotation you need to:

Go to your channel Video Manager

*Next to the video that you wish to edit, click the **down arrow** to the right of the Edit button and select **Annotations.***

*Click the **Add annotation** button on the right.*

*Click **Apply changes** when you've finished creating your annotations.*

Next you should be using an End Slate. An End Slate is the final screen at the end of the video which contains a selection of smaller embedded videos. The idea is to encourage the person viewing the video to click and watch another of the publisher's videos. Here's a link to Outromaker, a free online End Slate creator http://outromaker.com/.

Subscribe Button

To add a Subscribe button to each of your videos is again simple; to do this you need to create a 100x300px .png button which says '**Click Here to Subscribe**'. You then click Video Manager >Channel >Branding and upload your .png button as a watermark.

I always set the button to display throughout the entire video. You can also add a subscribe button to each video using annotations.

Advanced Twitter Tips and Tricks

In this chapter I will show you some cool Twitter applications and a few advanced tips which I have picked up along the way. Hopefully this chapter will take your existing Twitter skills to a new level!

Mentions Function

Let's begin by discussing the Twitter Mentions function; this is when you message a Twitter user in a tweet. For example, if I was to contact myself I would use '@darren_ackers – I love your social media book #socialmedia'. In this example I've mentioned myself and used the hashtag #socialmedia. When you do use the mentions feature, I strongly advise to use one or two hashtags which relate to your tweet. By adding hashtags your tweet will be seen by more Twitter users, and your tweet will go viral. Try this and see for yourself. Also, when you use the mention feature, always try to add a character before the @ sign. If you do not put a character before the @ sign, your tweet will only be seen by your followers. To solve this, place 'hi' or 'hello' before the @ sign – here's what it looks like 'Hi @darren_ackers, I love your social media book #socialmedia'. By do this, your tweet will be seen outside of your network.

Hashtags

Hashtags are imperative to include in your tweets, and more importantly, hashtags need to be aligned to the content of your tweet to maximize the viral potential of the tweet. The common hashtag rule is use one or two hashtags in a tweet; more than two hashtags are over kill and make a tweet look like spam. If you want your tweet to get noticed, only use one or two hashtags. To find popular hashtags and trending hashtags, I use the website Hashtagify http://hashtagify.me. Hashtagify is free to use and is a great online tool to help you discover hashtags to reach your audience. It will also show the top influencers who use a specific hashtag.

Advanced Searches

Twitter has a built in advanced search function which allows you to search across the Twitter platform using specific words and phrases. You use Twitter's advanced search to discover hashtags, people, places, dates and tweets. Here's the advanced search link: https://twitter.com/search-advanced?

Your Twitter Username

When you select your Twitter username, my advice is to keep it simple and select a username similar or the same as your name. For example, say you were a Sales Rep at Oracle and your username was something like 'Oracle_Sales_Pro'. You then built a network of Twitter followers and a few years later left Oracle and joined one of Oracle's competitors. You spent all that time building a Twitter network under a username associated with Oracle and the username 'Oracle_Sales_Pro' is now no good to you because you do not sell Oracle software.

Twitter Profile Picture

In my opinion, too many Twitter users use avatars or funny pictures as their profile picture. I don't understand why they cannot use a photograph of themselves. By adding a photo of yourself to your profile, your audience and followers will trust you more, and you will enjoy a better experience on Twitter. Furthermore, always take the advantage and customize your profile with a colorful background header. To edit your profile background, click the 'Edit Profile' button. Twitter recommends the header image to be 1500x1500 pixels and the profile photo to be 400x400 pixels. You should also add a bio to your profile of up to 160 characters and add your website, location and LinkedIn URL.

Twitter Lists

In 2009 Twitter added the 'Lists' feature, this change made it possible for users to create lists and add any Twitter user to a list. Lists are a good way to categorize your followers. Here's a tip for you, all lists can be made private or public. I recommend making all your lists private so no other user can view your list. It baffles me when I see lists made public and not private. After all, it can take months to create a Twitter list and by not making it private, any Twitter user can view a list and steal the list users for their own list. The 'Lists' feature is accessed by clicking on 'Profile and Settings' on the main menu. I'll now describe how I use lists working in sales.

I'm an advocate of social selling and use social media daily to source prospects and build relationships with prospects and clients. Each week I try to source lists which are public and subscribe to them. I do this to discover new prospective clients or useful Twitter users to follow. By subscribing to public lists I easily add new users to my private lists. To find out the lists a Twitter user is a member of, you need to visit their profile and click the 'Lists' option on the menu.

Another way to source prospective clients on Twitter is to subscribe to your competitors lists. You can then steal their list followers and add them to your list.

Here's a cool way to build Twitter Lists of prospective clients on autopilot using IFTTT.

In a previous chapter I discussed IFTTT (If This Then That) and how IFTTT uses recipes. I use a Recipe called 'Build a Twitter List from a specific #hashtag'. This recipe allows you to link a Twitter List to IFTTT and when someone uses a specific hashtag on Twitter, IFTTT fires up and adds this user to the list you specified on autopilot. Then you need to go through your list and remove any users which are not of interest to you. Let me give you an example on how to use this process when a conference or big event is going on.

There was a conference which happened in 2014 organized by the Chartered Institute of Personnel Development and some of the attendees were potential customers who I would like to engage with and get to know. The hashtag #CIPD14 was used to promote the conference. I set up the IFTTT Recipe called 'Build a Twitter List from a specific #hashtag' and used the #CIPD14 hashtag. Luckily for me a number of potential customers began tweeting about the conference using the hashtag #CIPD14 and my Twitter list began to fill up with prospects.

As you can see, I gathered a number of prospective clients on autopilot. All I had to do was follow them and engage with them on Twitter. A word of advice here, never pitch a prospective client straight away, always engage with them first and build a relationship before asking for a meeting or pitching your product to them. Always help your contacts and engage with them in the first instance – earn their trust. Another big no no is to send a promotional or sales message straight to your connection using Twitter's Direct Message feature.

The best way to engage with your prospective clients on Twitter is to retweet, share and favorite their tweets. Send them interesting articles or pieces of content which will interest them. You can also connect your prospects with each other by tweeting an image or infographic. You can then tag up to 10 of your prospects to the image. I've had success by creating an attractive infographic to a tweet and then tagging a few prospects to this infographic tweet asking them what they think.

Tweroid
Tweroid is a free online application that helps take the guess work out of the best time to tweet. Like I said before, knowing the times your followers are on Twitter dramatically increases the chances of retweets and mentions. This service works by analyzing your past 200 tweets, your followers' tweets and those you follow. You then generate a report on the Tweroid dashboard and sync the data with Buffer. Buffer will then automatically schedule your tweets so they coincide when your followers are active on Twitter. Unfortunately the

free Tweroid version is limited to 1,000 followers so you will need to pay a small sum each month to use this service when you have more than 1,000 followers.

Unfollowers.com

Unfollowers.com is a cool free Twitter and Instagram application accessed through a web browser. What I like about unfollowers.com is the easy on the eye dashboard where you can instantly see who is not following you back. In addition, they include free automated tools which allows you to create auto direct messages and welcome tweets on autopilot.

Furthermore, you can easily manage your Twitter lists and view your Twitter stats over the past few weeks. The majority of features are available to use at no cost, however you can unlock advanced features by subscribing to their 'Premium Service'. Another useful feature you can use is the 'Add a Source', this permits you to track someone's Twitter account so you can identify who they follow, who follows them and their unfollowers. I use this specific feature to source new followers who could be potentially prospects for me to forge relationships with.

TweetReach.com

TweetReach is developed by an American software vendor and the application is widely used by many marketing agencies and marketers around the globe. TweetReach is free to use, but it also has a paid monthly subscription. I use the free version. I like this application because it gives great insights on hashtags, top contributors, Twitter users, how far your tweet traveled and more. If you search on a Twitter user, the application will display insights such as who retweeted a tweet, users who mentioned this user and a list of tweets by user. For me, it lets me know what a prospect is saying on Twitter and gives me insights on problems and issues they are experiencing. Also, by entering a hashtag, you can find new followers who use specific hashtags. Furthermore, you will gather insights such as activity and lists of tweets containing specific hashtags.

Social Bro

Social Bro is a free Twitter analytic online dashboard which is accessed through a web browser. There is an upgrade version which isn't free, but the no cost version has sufficient functionality for my needs. In brief, SocialBro is a data mining tool which offers a huge amount of information about your Twitter account. One of the solutions it offers is to let you know the time of day your Twitter contacts send their tweets. SocialBro also integrates with Buffer so you can schedule your tweets. Because SocialBro lets you know the best time to tweet, you can then schedule your tweets through Buffer to match the best times to tweet. If your Klout score is important to you, then having your tweets retweeted and read will increase your score.

Pay with a Tweet: Social Payment in a Social Networking World

In a world where social capital is king and everyone is scrambling for attention, Pay with a Tweet http://www.paywithatweet.com/ offers entrepreneurs, creative minds and established businesses a way to reach out to a media-saturated audience.

The concept behind Pay with a Tweet is simple. A single button is installed on your website, and when a browser clicks on it, they are given the chance to create a Tweet or a Facebook post about your content. As soon as they have done so, they are granted access to a download that you provide.

At the most basic level, Pay with a Tweet offers your browsers and potential clients something concrete and valuable for something that they perceive as very simple. Essentially, all you are asking them to do is something that they would be doing anyway, just slightly modified for your needs. However, much like a single snowball can cause an avalanche, a single Tweet from one person can reach dozens of their friends who in turn continue the pattern.

Programs like Twitter and Facebook hold our social interactions together. They give us a face-to-face immediacy with friends, family and colleagues that we do not see every day, and the personal nature of these interactions lends them authority. As the content creator, you can reach a certain number of people with your own Tweets, but the number that your combined followers can reach by contacting their followers is exponentially greater!

One of the great benefits of Pay with a Tweet is that it relies on completely natural social patterns. You are not asking people to sell your product or to advertise it. Instead, you are only asking them to do something very simple and you are rewarding them with something that they want.

What are some of the things that you can offer with Pay with a Tweet?

For example, if you are company that retails products, you may offer a coupon that grants the bearer 20% off their next purchase. The value is clear, and most people would be willing to make a Tweet for the concrete reward of a reduced price.

Pay with a Tweet also allows you to offer free samples of your own creative work. If you are advertising for a band, a Tweet could result in the download of a free song or a brief interview video with the band itself. Similarly, authors can use Pay with a Tweet to offer a free story or a sample chapter that is not available elsewhere. If you are an instructor of some kind, the download might consist of a free video lesson or a written tutorial.

How I Use Pay for a Tweet to Promote Clickbank Affiliate Products

I write a short How to eBook in the same niche as the product and use this as a free giveaway. I create my product promotional affiliate link Tweet on Pay for a Tweet and copy the iFrame code for the button. I then set up a squeeze page on my blog and advertise the free eBook I created. I explain that the visitor can download this eBook if they click the Pay for a Tweet or Pay with a Facebook Post. They click the button, share my Tweet; boom, my Tweet goes viral. All I have to do is drive traffic to my squeeze page.

In a time when the Internet is swamped with things like pay-per-click ads and flashing banners, Pay with a Tweet tells your browsers that they are important to you and that you are not going to push anything on them. Research and plain common sense tells us that people hate to feel like they are being forced into anything; complicated click-through traffic and requests for additional contacts creates feelings of resentment and anger.

On the other hand, Pay with a Tweet offers a clear exchange. You are asking for a very simple, very basic and practically cost-free type of promotion from your browser, and in exchange, you are offering something of value to them. This is one of the most honest win-win exchanges out there when you are looking for advertising.

When you are thinking about how to get Pay with a Tweet working for you, just start by thinking of the reward. The reward can be anything that interests your clients, whether it is a small piece of writing, a single song, a coupon or an exclusive image. Once you have the reward in mind, you are ready to institute the Pay with a Tweet system. The program is easy and intuitive, allowing you to call the shots on your own media advertising campaign.

With more than 10,000 Pay with a Tweet buttons created and more than 400,000 files downloaded, the first social payment program has proven that it can get you the attention and the sales that you have been looking for!

Livestreaming Apps Made for Twitter

At the time of writing this part to my book, there are 2 new cool apps which are gathering pace and causing a storm in the social media world. These apps are Meerkat and Periscope (acquired by Twitter); easy to use iPhone apps which both stream live video to a user's Twitter account. You could say it's a video selfie. Simply put, both apps allow the user to broadcast real time video through their phone and then other Twitter users can watch this video feed and comment with tweets that the broadcaster can see and respond to. The other problem with live streaming is the attraction of privacy. For example, in May 2015 Floyd Mayweather and Manny Pacquiao fought each other in one of the biggest financial boxing bouts in Vegas. The typical price to watch the fight at home was $100, but anyone who watched the fight was able to live stream this match to their Twitter feed and others could watch the fight for free.

These apps are reasonably similar to each other, albeit different user interfaces, but the major difference for me is Meerkat allows you to schedule broadcasts for a later date and Periscope does not. What I do find annoying with Meerkat is the way it automatically tweets a link to your broadcast as soon as you begin broadcasting. Periscope gives you the option to tell the world when you broadcast or not tell the world when you broadcast. Sometimes you might want to keep your broadcast private, but with Meerkat you cannot stream privately.

You might be asking how to use Meerkat or Periscope to market a business. If you're a business you could live stream: how to use your product, product demonstration, Q&As about your product/ service and stream a training video. Remember Periscope is now owned by Twitter so my guess is it will increase in popularity and be the number one streaming app for Twitter. My advice is to try both Periscope and Meerkat and decide which is best for you.

Here's a great article on the Get Response blog which provides some useful tips on using Periscope for business: http://blog.getresponse.com/20-unmissable-tips-for-using-periscope-for-business.html

Social Selling Case Study

I thought I would share with you a strategy I use in my day to day sales job. You may have heard of, or be familiar with the buzz phrase 'social selling'. Social selling is described as a sales tool, sales approach, sales methodology...call it what you want... where you use social channels (Twitter, LinkedIn, Facebook etc) to build relationships with prospective customers. Simply put, you find out which social channels your prospect uses and then you engage with them on that social channel(s).

I've had great success prospecting on Twitter and then moving the relationship off Twitter and onto LinkedIn. I spend most of my social media time on LinkedIn. I will now share with you a social selling method I use using Twitter and break the process down into bullet points:

This actual prospect in question was a senior buyer at a FTSE 100 listed retailer.

- Found prospect on Twitter from a competitors Twitter list
- Took photo of an item I bought which the retailer sold
- Posted the photo on Twitter together with a few words commenting on the great customer service I received from the retailer
- I included the prospects Twitter handle and the retailers Twitter handle using the @ mentions feature

- The prospect replied back to me and the retailer favorited my tweet
- I engaged with the prospect on Twitter a few more times over a week
- I then asked them if I could send over a document outlining a training course we provided and described how it could solve a challenge they had
- I contacted the prospect and asked if we could meet to discuss this further – they agreed
- I met them and we had a great meeting because we had formed a relationship. The prospect became a client and bought our training.

How to Find a Prospective Customers Email Address

The following paragraphs may be helpful if you work in a job where you contact prospective clients by email to introduce your product or service. I've been in sales for most of my working life and I have always enjoyed finding new prospects and reaching out to them. Depending on the type of prospect you want to contact, sometimes email is the best way to begin building relationships with them. I sell to Corporate senior makers who travel often and we find email is the best communication tool when we do not know their direct telephone numbers.

Let's say I found a prospective customer on LinkedIn and my objective is to get a meeting with them. To make this easy to demonstrate, let's say this fictitious person is John Dean at JP Morgan. Here are the steps I use to find a person's corporate email address:

- Type JP Morgan in Google to find the format of the domain name
- Use www.email-format.com to find out the format JP Morgan uses which is typically firstname.lastname@jpmorgan.com. Alternatively I could have Google search 'email@jpmorgan.com' to find out the email format
- I now want to check to see if this email is valid. To do this, I use an email verification website such as www.verifyemailaddress.org. These verification websites will test the recipient's mail server and check if the email

address exists – this validation check is performed in seconds. Most email verification websites are free and they make money when you upload multiple email addresses in bulk to verify. Uploading bulk email addresses is a good idea when you want to clean email lists to reduce the number of hard bounces with email campaigns. Spam monitoring services frown upon multiple hard bounces as it signals spam; if this happens your domain could get penalized and be added to a spam list which means your email will be blocked when sending to certain domains.

- That's it, you should now know if john.dean@jpmorgan.com is a valid email.

LinkedIn Tricks

Too many LinkedIn users think that their profile should be designed and formatted like a resume. Before you create your LinkedIn profile you need to decide the purpose and objectives you want to achieve from your profile. For example, is your objective one of the following: are you looking for a job and want recruiters to find you, are you looking to attract prospective clients, are you simply looking to build your business network and so on.

Before I share my LinkedIn profile tips with you, please ensure you have a professional photo of yourself, preferably a headshot, uploaded to your profile. If you do not have a professional photo of yourself on your profile, then I can guarantee you are wasting your time on LinkedIn. Without a photo of yourself other LinkedIn users will be deterred from connecting with you and think you are not a real person. A missing profile photo signals that this LinkedIn user is not genuine and is hiding something. This also applies to other social media platforms.

LinkedIn Profile Tips

1. Turn off your activity broadcast so that your connections cannot see you are updating your profile. To turn off your activity broadcast click on your privacy settings and change the setting 'Select who can see your activity' to 'only you'.
2. Your profile headline should not just be your job title. Make the profile title interesting and include adjectives, and focus on what makes you different. Think like a client of yours and imagine what they would like to read. Moreover, think about

the solutions and the problems you can solve. Think about how you help clients.

3. Customize your profile URL from the standard LinkedIn URL. Customize the URL to your name; my custom profile URL is https://uk.linkedin.com/in/darrenackers. To change and customize your profile URL go to Settings > Edit Profile > Customize Your Public URL.

4. Connect your LinkedIn account with your Twitter account. By doing this will give you the option to share your LinkedIn updates simultaneously on Twitter and give more exposure to your updates. When you post direct to Twitter from LinkedIn, always try to include one or two hashtags to your update.

5. Summary sections of your profile – always sell yourself and explain clearly how you help your clients. Do not fall into the trap of stating your achievements as viewers of your profile will be turned off. Also, ensure you include a number of keywords in the summary so you appear on searches. I use bullet points and list my keywords under a subtitle which I name 'Specialisms'.

6. Complete your job history and all the profile fields which you can. Your objective is to thoroughly complete your profile and achieve 'All Star Status'. LinkedIn will reward you with 'All Star Status' once your profile is complete.

7. Upload rich content and media to your profile such as white papers, video, slideshare's etc.

8. Follow LinkedIn Influencers by visiting LinkedIn Pulse. These influencers you follow will be displayed on your profile.

9. Add skills to the 'Skills' section on your profile. Remember to order them so your priority skills are at the top.
10. Avoid over used words in your profile that lack substance such as creative, effective, strategic, patient, expert, driven, motivated and analytical. If you chose to use some of these words, my advice is to use them sparingly.
11. Reach out and ask for recommendations from your network. Be brazen and send recommendation requests to people who know you well.

Whilst we are discussing LinkedIn profiles, I never connect with LinkedIn users who have either of the following since I feel they are not fit to join my network. They are:

- Someone with no connections (harsh I know).
- Profile with no photo.
- Profile with company logo as the photo.
- Profiles which contain lots of phone numbers, social media profiles and email addresses.

I strongly believe you should always be building your network and connecting to new users daily. My advice is to be careful and do not connect with the objective of having the largest possible network and thousands of connections. Connecting on LinkedIn is not a competition.

LinkedIn Pulse

I discussed 'Pulse' by LinkedIn in a previous chapter to generate content for sharing. Pulse is also a great source to develop you and learn from others through reading their published articles. Pulse is also a great way to keep up to date with industry news. I use the Pulse IOS app on my iPhone to read articles whilst travelling on the train. If I read an article worth sharing with my network, I simply press the share button on my iPhone and voila – the article is shared on my LinkedIn and Twitter accounts.

Publishing Your Own Articles on Pulse

LinkedIn allows users to post an article on Pulse so that any LinkedIn user can read this article. Moreover, your LinkedIn network will get notified about your article. To post an article simply click the pencil to the right of your 'share' box. Obviously ensure your article is well written and is grammatically correct. You will find that posting your articles on Pulse achieves more engagement and views than sharing your articles on your LinkedIn timeline as an update. If the article you post on Pulse is from your blog, always add the blog post URL to the article to encourage readers to visit your blog. This may sound common sense, but I can guarantee few Pulse publishers actually include and promote their blog in a post. Another tip is to publish your article in LinkedIn groups where you are a member. And finally make sure you share your LinkedIn article on Twitter and other social media channels.

LinkedIn Groups

I think many business owners forget the power of LinkedIn groups to market a product or service. Of course you can join up to 50 groups which LinkedIn allows and you can set up your own group. When you set up a group the temptation is to promote and sell your product or service. By doing this, your group members will most likely leave your group, and then it will become increasingly difficult to sell to these prospective clients in the future.

If you are serious about creating a successful group, my advice is to use your group as a 'thought leadership' vehicle. You want your customers and prospective customers to recognize you as a thought leader and therefore a person who they should trust and come to for advice. Get into the habit of sharing and post interesting articles and content in your group. Use your group to post your own thought leadership, case studies or other documents which will be of use to your audience. Once your group is up and running, you will find the group members will begin posting articles and questions of their own for the group to answer.

When group members begin posting new threads and commenting in your group, you will learn what is challenging them and discover the issues they are experiencing. When I discover their challenges, I try and suggest a useful article or piece of research which will address their challenge. Moreover, when your group becomes established, you can use the group 'Promotion' feature like you would use email marketing to send the group members emails. The Promotion feature allows you to send a direct message to the group members and this message will not be displayed on the group.

Here are a few tips on using the Group Settings of your group:

Members of this group

I recommend you to set this to 'Free to post comments only and submit everything else'. By using this setting all new group threads will require your permission to post. When a group member posts a new thread in my group, I send them a thank you note and explain their new thread is now live. This is a great to build relationships with your group members.

Also set the group joining setting to 'Request to Join'. Users must request to join the group and be approved by a manager. Always use this setting to control who joins your group. The last thing you need is to let competitors in to your group or individuals who will post spam or rude comments.

Templates

LinkedIn allows all group owners to create standard templates (found in group settings) which are used when new members join the group and are sent to users who you decline membership to. Without doubt, the 'Welcome Message' is the best template. This template you should treat as an auto responder, by this I mean create a template which welcomes the group member but also lets them know more about you, product or company. In your template message always include a link to your newsletter, your other social profiles and ask them to connect with you on LinkedIn.

Here a few more general LinkedIn tips

Inmail – LinkedIn allows you to contact other users. So, when you use the free or paid version of LinkedIn, always try to use your monthly allocating Inmail allowance. I use Inmail when I cannot work out the LinkedIn users email address. I always prefer to work out a LinkedIn users email address so I can then capture it in an Excel spreadsheet. I have worked with sales people who solely rely on using Inmail to reach out to prospective customers. For me this is lazy and corner cutting. The advantage of having a prospective clients email address is that you can email them more often and you can add them to Excel lists and include them in mail merges. Moreover, Inmail doesn't allow you to include graphics in the email whereas mail merges do.

Saved Search – the Save Search function is found on the Advanced Search screen. The Save Search function allows you save specific searches to find jobs or people. I have a paid LinkedIn account and I can save thirteen searches. The main advantages of saving searches is LinkedIn will email you regular results with new users to approach and it saves a bundle of time when searching for new connections because it saves you completing all the search fields. The search function also allows you to monitor companies and competition by tracking their new employees.

Linked Tags – the LinkedIn Tags feature allows you to organize your connections in groups. The easiest way to add tags is by visiting a LinkedIn users profile and click on the Relationship tab which is normally directly below the users profile photograph. In the Relationship tab you will see the Tag feature where you can add new tags and add the user to a specific tag.

Who viewed your profile – found under Profile, this function lets you see who has had a peek at your profile. I treat these peeking users as warm leads and always send them a personalized connection request. I make a conscientious effort to regularly visit prospective clients' profiles and hope they then look at my profile. When they look at my profile I will send them a personalized connection request thanking them for looking at my profile. A cool LinkedIn app which we use at my company is 'Autopilot for LinkedIn' – here's the URL https://autopilotforlinkedin.com/.

Autopilot for LinkedIn
Autopilot for LinkedIn works in the background using either Google Chrome or Firefox browsers. Once installed you perform an advanced search on LinkedIn and Autopilot begins by viewing the profiles in your advanced search. What I like is you can use a LinkedIn advanced search to forensically target prospective clients by job role, industry and location. Once Autopilot on LinkedIn sees your advanced search, it starts viewing a maximum of 750 LinkedIn profiles daily. Statistics show that between 6% and 8% of these people who had their profile viewed will visit the profile of the person who visited their profile. So, if this application views 700 LinkedIn profiles on your behalf, 50 LinkedIn users could look at your profile. Obviously before signing up to Autopilot on LinkedIn, it's imperative you have created a great LinkedIn profile.

Connecting on LinkedIn - Quick Tip
If you have sent multiple connection requests to LinkedIn users, you most likely have seen the pop up message which asks you to enter

the persons email address. If you do not know the persons email address then please read on...I have a cool work around. Download the LinkedIn App to your iPhone or Android phone and search for this person and press the 'Connect' button, or preferably send a personalized message asking them to connect. For some reason, the app overrides the need to enter the persons email address.

If you have the time, I always suggest that any message to connect on LinkedIn should be personalized. To send a personalized message through the iPhone app, you need to visit the persons profile and click the three dots in the top right corner. A pop box is displayed and you can select the 'Customize invite' link to send a personalized message. Sending a personalized connection request message is straight forward when using a PC or laptop. All you do is click on the 'Connect' button on the LinkedIn user's profile and type your message.

Did you know you can follow LinkedIn users who are not connections?

LinkedIn allows you to follow 2nd and 3rd degree connections. To follow a 2nd or 3rd degree connection, click the 'Send Inmail' button on the persons profile and choose 'Follow'. Now you can see their updates on LinkedIn and engage with them without being a 1st degree connection.

Facebook Page Tips

A Facebook page can be a powerful social marketing tool when you know how to use it properly, however, to get the most from a FB Page, you have to be on top of it and regularly post useful and interesting content to keep your readers engaged. With a lack of fresh content your readers will disengage and your efforts will not be fruitful. You should consider a FB Page as a mini website for your business or product; a shop window to capture the interest of current and future customers. The trick is to keep your readers hooked and keep coming back to see what's new on your page.

Here are my Facebook Page tips:

Claim Your Vanity URL

By default, Facebook will create an ugly looking URL for a FB Page. You need a minimum of 25 'likes' and be an admin to customize the URL. Keep your custom URL simple and related to your business, product or brand. Once you have 25 'likes' for your page you need to visit www.facebook.com/username and follow the wizard to set up the vanity URL. Remember that once set up, neither username nor vanity URL can be changed. Therefore think what the vanity URL will say and relate it to your business or product.

Page Description and Header Image

Complete the description and profile for your page and include keywords and phrases related to your business in the description. Adding keywords and phrases to your description is imperative to show up in the Facebook organic page search results. Use a high resolution image for your page header and the optimal size for the header image is approximately 851x315 pixels.

Follow Other Facebook Pages

I recommend following competitors FB Pages and leading brands in a similar sector to yours to get a feel how they engage with their followers. Moreover, to see how they use their page and the type of content they publish. Remember top brands employ a dedicated social media team and these experts will be trained in the latest digital marketing techniques to engage and build their brands online. Also, don't be afraid to comment (not spam) on your competitors page as their followers could get curious and visit your page. Remember that your Facebook profile will always be displayed when you comment and not your FB Page image.

Engaging with Followers

Before you can engage with your followers, your page must be full of useful content which is of value to your followers. Once your page is full of content you should let your friends, family, work colleagues and social media connections aware of your page. Your focus here is to ask them to share and like your page so your page appears on their social timelines. Publish surveys and ask your followers questions to encourage engagement. Publish exclusive discount codes and offers. Add photos of your team or photos of your office. Moreover, add photos, stories and videos of your happy customers. Your best sales people are your happy customers (quote from Jill Rowley, the Queen of Social Selling).

A great way to gain new followers is by running a competition for an iPad, Apple Watch or something people would like to own. You then explain that to win the prize, all entrants need to like and follow your page. This strategy also works well on LinkedIn too to promote a company page. Finally, monitor your FB Page regularly to see which posts your followers prefer and respond to.

Respond to Comments

Always respond to comments whether good or bad and never delete comments. Thank followers who leave comments, offer them your help and always reply to negative comments. Do not get into an argument with any negative commenter and try to turn any negative situation into a positive one.

Schedule Your Posts

Facebook allows you to schedule all posts to your page which is a useful feature. For example, on a Monday you could create seven page posts and schedule them to be posted each day of the week. Publishing fresh daily content is a great way to build a following.

Followers Ask Questions

Encourage your followers to ask questions by publishing posts which you ask for their opinion or advice. Ask your followers to send you questions about issues and challenges they have. With this approach, you will ask for your followers to send you questions and you will record a YouTube video answering their question. Then you will publish the YouTube video back on your Facebook page and share it across your other social platforms. Recording a YouTube video to answer a question is an easy method to create content for your Facebook page and a simple way to spread the word.

Add a Link to Your Website and Social Accounts

Get into the habit of placing a Facebook logo on your website and link it to your Facebook page. Also, add your FB page link to your other social account profiles.

Getting More 'Likes'

Here's a quick tip which will help you get new Twitter followers and people to 'like' your Facebook Page. For this tip to work you need to visit blogs to find great articles/ content or look on YouTube for awesome videos to share. The trick is to share the article/ content or video as a tweet on Twitter. Before you publish your tweet, you need to find out the authors or YouTube users Twitter handle. Most blogs will display the author's Twitter handle and the same can be said about the YouTube users channel profile.

Once you have their Twitter handle, make sure you give credit to this person by including and mentioning their Twitter handle in the tweet. The person will be notified by Twitter that you have tweeted about their video or article and this Twitter person will more than likely thank you on Twitter. Twitter will now notify you about this person thanking you. Since you have done them a favor by sharing their article or video, now is a good time to ask them to repay the favor by following you and liking your Facebook page.

Facebook Advertising Tips

Why use Facebook advertising?

Facebook has a user base in the excess of 8 billion global users and is the only online advertising platform which offers precision targeting of new customers. You can target new and current customers by age, gender, and location, their interests and specific devices they use – tablets, phones and pc. Moreover, you can create marketing campaigns to target narrow or broad audiences. Before I give you a few tips on Facebook advertising, you will need to know the following information to prevent you wasting money on your Facebook advertising. You need to know; who you want to target by gender, location, age and ideally their interests. Like any marketing campaign, you need to track and measure your results to work out what works and what doesn't work.

When you're ready go to www.facebook.com/business and on this page you will find useful short videos on using Facebook adverts. Please take your time and watch these videos.

Creating Your Advert

When creating any pay per click (PPC) ad, you should use simple words (less is more) and a clear call to action to tell the user what to do next. Example call to actions: 'click here to see the offer', 'click to grab your copy today', 'only a few remaining, buy today'.

Facebook ads allow you to upload a video or multiple images. I prefer to upload the maximum six images allowed so when my ad runs, different images will be displayed and I can then understand which image converts in to a sale the best. This is great when I'm deciding and testing which cover I should use for my published eBooks. Here are more tips:

- Use high quality and eye catching images.
- Try and use funny images related to your product or business.
- Customize your ad headline and text as Facebook will automatically create a headline and text for you.
- Experiment with ad positions across the ad types such as Newsfeed, Mobile Newsfeed, and Desktop Right Column. The Newsfeed ad is displayed in the user timeline and tends to be more expensive, but you do receive more clicks than the right column position.
- Experiment and split test with different types of advert designs.
- Include a discount offer in your advert and see what happens.
- Add a video of happy customer to the advert.
- Try an advert with multiple images called the carousel.
- Create a dedicated landing page on your website for your advert.
- Create and test a variety of landing pages and test which page is better. Then understand why the landing page performs better and keep tweaking it to get the optimal landing page.
- The right column, which is displayed on the right side of the screen, tends to be cheaper because they are less

prominent and receive less clicks than the timeline adverts. That said, right column adverts can produce great results. My advice for using right column adverts is to ensure you take your time designing the advert and consistently test to see which advert performs the best. Done correctly, the right column desktop advert can produce a solid return on investment.

- The optimal advert size for the newsfeed position is approximately 1200x628 pixels.
- In the pricing section, Facebook will set your bid price by default. Change these settings so you set the amount you're willing to pay per click and control your costs.
- Control what you spend by setting the budget to daily or lifetime. Daily will cap what you spend in a day and lifetime will control your total budget for that campaign. Watch out because each campaign you create has its own budget.
- Use the Daily Reach and Audience Definition to see approximately how many people you will reach with your advert.
- If you are looking to attract local customers or own a retail shop, please make sure you only target your local area using the selections in New Audience. Here you can select your advert to be displayed based on country, city, postcode, age, gender, interests and languages.

Custom Audiences

Customer Audiences is a unique feature only available to Facebook. Customer Audiences allows you to target lists of people who you want to see your advert. This is extremely effective because you simply upload a list of contacts and Facebook will only display your advert to these contacts. These contacts could be your customers, prospective customers and customers who have bought from you in the past. Another option is to create a 'Lookalike Audience' which finds and targets new customers. This works by analyzing who 'liked' your Facebook page and then will target Facebook users who have similar interests.

Conversion Tracking

Conversion Tracking works by recording who has visited your web page directly from your Facebook advert and makes a purchase. For this to work you need to install a piece of HTML code, called a Pixel, to the payment page on your website. When a referral from your Facebook advert makes a purchase on your website, the pixel fires and will send a signal to Facebook and you will see the data in your advertising account.

Facebook - Join Free Groups

Join Facebook groups and even better, start your own group on Facebook. The great advantage about FB groups is it's 100% free and you can create an unlimited number of groups. Use groups sensibly, and my advice is not to get carried away since it can take up a lot of your time to manage FB groups.

You can have an open group that anyone can join, as your company or product shop window on Facebook. Once you have Facebook members who join your group, you can contact them instantly by sending them a message through Facebook.

The other option is have a closed group, this way your members need your permission to join and your group is not visible to the whole world. A closed group is ideal if you are sharing confidential information that you don't want your competitors to see.

The final option is a secret group, this is only visible to Facebook users you invite. In the past I have used a secret group for employees and for my directors to communicate with each other.

Here's a link which provides more details about these types of groups.

https://www.facebook.com/help/www/220336891328465

Instagram Tips and Tricks

Facebook knew exactly what they were doing when they bought Instagram for $1billion. Since the purchase, the number of users has flocked to Instagram and its growth has been exponential. Instagram has over 75 million daily users. What's most interesting is that over 50% of Instagram users are aged between 18-29 and Women are fractionally the popular user compared to Men.

Here are my Instagram tips.

Profile and Bio

Complete it fully and upload a high resolution photograph which is similar to the image you use on other social platforms. Add your other social profile links such as Twitter, LinkedIn and Facebook Page.

Posting Photographs and Images

Post a mix of business and funny photos/ images to make your account interesting and encourage followers to 'like' to your photos/ images. Remember to post photos and images related to your business, product or service. To upload your photos/ images you can use a web browser or Android or IOS App. I prefer to upload photos/ images using my iPhone as I find this method convenient whilst on the go. If you are a business, you could post photos of your product, amusing photos of your employees, photos of your team fundraising, videos of how to use your product and videos of happy customers talking about your product or service.

You should consistently monitor the 'likes' for your photos and videos on Instagram because this will give you insight and what content your followers enjoy.

How to Increase Your Followers

Most importantly you should post interesting content to Instagram. You should engage with your followers and other users by commenting and liking their photos, videos and images. Follow other Instagram users who you follow you on Twitter, Facebook, and LinkedIn etc. Share your Instagram photos and videos across your other social profiles. An easy method to share is to create an Instagram IFTTT Recipe to automate sharing from your Instagram account. Try these Recipes:

Instagram to Facebook

Instagram to Facebook Page

Instagram to Twitter

Instagram to LinkedIn

By setting all these recipes you will post an Instagram photo or video and it will be shared to Facebook, Twitter and LinkedIn on autopilot. Many switched on brands will post videos on Instagram and embed the link on their Facebook Page and then use Facebook advertising to make the video appear on Facebook user's timelines. The Facebook user will see the advert in their timeline and out of curiosity visit the original video on Instagram and follow the brand.

Get into the habit of embedding your Instagram content on your website and blog. To get the embed code; simply click on the three dots in the right corner. Another good trick is to offer discount codes and rewards to encourage new followers.

Use Trending Hashtags

Unlike Twitter, it is acceptable to use multiple hashtags on Instagram content. Use relevant hashtags to your business and product and always include popular, trending hashtags. Trending hashtags include: #love, #me, #selfie, #cute, #follow, #happy, #like, #fun and #smile. Please search Google to find more popular hashtags. Here's a great resource to find top Instagram hashtags http://top-hashtags.com/instagram/.

Managing Followers

Any experienced Instagram user will know that you cannot view your followers or who you follow on Instagram.com. To view your followers and who follows you, you will need the IOS or Android App. You can also get these insights at websta.me and unfollowgram.com. I prefer unfollowgram.com as it shows who unfollowed you and those who do not follow you which you follow.

SlideShare Presentation Advice

SlideShare is another social site where you can upload a PDF or Power Point presentation for free. Once your document is uploaded, you then share this on your Twitter, Pinterest, LinkedIn, Facebook page, or other social media platforms or sites. Can you see now how SlideShare can easily go viral once you've created an upload?

When I create a SlideShare Power Point presentation for my author business, I like to add my Author Page URL to each slide. Later on I will show you how to set up a domain name and how to redirect this domain name to another URL. Redirect domains are great if you need to disguise an ugly URL.

My advice is to create Power Point presentations with 7-10 slides and talk about the problems your product or service solves. Then talk about the pain and the implications which your customers experience because of their problems. Finally talk about your product's features and how they solve the problems which you talked about earlier.

SlideShare was bought by LinkedIn, so you can now add your SlideShare presentation to your LinkedIn profile. To do this login in to your LinkedIn account, click Profile, then click Edit Profile. Now scroll down and click Add Link where you want the presentation to be displayed. Add your SlideShare presentation link and LinkedIn will upload your presentation to your LinkedIn profile. You can also do the same with any YouTube videos. It only takes a few minutes and is well worth your effort.

Article Directories

Article Directories are not quite as effective as they once were. Google saw to that with their algorithm updates, such as the Farmer, the Penguin, and the Panda. In saying this, the top article sites, such as EzineArticles.com and GoArticles.com still hold a high page rank and enjoy a large number of daily visitors.

My suggestion is to join up for free and post 500-600 word articles that are associated with your product or service.

Publishing an article is straightforward. You can include two links in the resource box. I always link each article to my Amazon Author page and my blog darrenackers.com. Another option is to link to your free gift to capture email addresses. I will cover this later on in the Aweber tutorial section for list building.

When you sign up for an article directory, I suggest you always complete the profile section. For example, EzineArticles allows you to create a personal URL, blog URL, Facebook fan page URL, Pinterest URL, and your eBook's ISBN. Creating an eBook is another marketing strategy which I will discuss later.

EzineArticles Tips

EzineArticles.com offers some awesome extra resources and Wordpress widgets. Once you are logged in, click on the Resources tab and you will see six resources. My favorite is the WordPress plugin. Let me tell you why.

- Your blog posts get automatically published on EzineArticles at the click of a button.

- Your saved resource boxes on EzineArticles can be used.

- You can republish older blog articles with ease.

- Select which of your author profiles to use per article.

- Monitor the status of your articles on EzineArticles.

Warning: If you are carrying out SEO on your site or blog, please do not publish the exact articles on your blog to EzineArticles straight away. Publish your articles on your blog first then, say after seven days, publish on EzineArticles. This way Google should credit your blog as the original article, therefore, won't penalize you for duplicate content. The ultra-safe way is to create a unique version of your blog post for EzineArticles.

Fiverr Gigs – Everything for Only 5 Bucks

For $5 you will be amazed at the services on offer at Fiverr.com. Fiverr is a global online marketplace where sellers offer a multitude of services for a surprisingly number of tasks. These are known as gigs. To promote your product or service, I suggest using Fiverr to find sellers who offer Facebook, Twitter, and video trailer gigs.

I can recommend Natalia on Fiverr http://fiverr.com/around86. She offers many gigs that will help authors. When I discuss writing an eBook later, this paragraph will make perfect sense.

I use her to format my books for Smashwords and occasionally Createspace when I'm feeling lazy. I find Smashwords formatting a real pain in the bum, so by paying Natalia a few dollars I will be confident that my book will be accepted on Smashwords premium. Again, Smashwords premium will be discussed later. If you are not using eBooks in your marketing arsenal, I feel sure you will enjoy that paragraph in this book.

Facebook Gigs

Promote your product or service to their 10,000+ followers on their Facebook timeline. Buy a $50 Facebook ad coupon on Fiverr to promote your product or service on Facebook Ads.

Twitter Gigs

Promote your product or service to their 61,000+ Twitter followers using different tweets. I use a guy called Tony Maria on Fiverr to tweet about my books. Another gig you can buy is to create a professional Twitter background for your profile.

Video Trailer

Create a 5-minute video trailer of your product or service that you can then embed on your blog using YouTube.

Squidoo and Hub Pages

Squidoo.com and HubPages.com are sites where you can build a hub or lens and publish content that is related to your business. Publish unique content, provide value, and then you can create a link to your website or blog. These sites receive a large number of daily visitors so this makes them great sites to promote a product or service.

What I like about HubPages is that you can create a capsule and link it with an Amazon Associates account. The Amazon affiliate link should point to your product, if it's listed on Amazon. If you are not familiar with Amazon Associates, here's the link: https://affiliate-program.amazon.com. If your product is listed on Amazon, all you do is drive traffic to your HubPage and each visitor will see your product listed on the Amazon section of your HubPage.

Pinterest Pin Your Images – Don't Forget Slideshare

Pinterest is a social website where you can bookmark images. You can set up different boards and post any image you choose on the board. You can add your Twitter profile and Facebook profile so that all your activity will be shared on your timelines.

Pinterest has a huge following, so you can engage with prospective readers by promoting your product or service. Just like Facebook, Pinterest members can "like" your pinned images. A technique I use is to pin my SlideShare presentations on Pinterest. Each slideshow presentation will show an excerpt of my book to whet their appetite.

As a marketing strategy you could create a SlideShare presentation and include a slide selling your free gift which could be a video or eBook. Place the URL link to your free gift and use your Squeeze Page (I will discuss later on) to capture your prospects email address. Then you can use your Aweber autoresponder (again this will be discussed later) to build a deep relationship with your prospect.

Scribd

Scribd is a free sharing social website where you can upload a range of documents in various different formats and then share them. This is a great place to upload content, attract prospective readers and allows you to place a link directly to your website or blog and again include your free gift URL within the document. As described on the previous page, you can then use Aweber to build relationships using an autoresponder.

It only takes five minutes to create an uploaded document, so it's real easy to use Scribd to promote your product or service. When you upload a document to Scribd I suggest your content should give advice and tips - basically don't upload a sales pitch, keep it simple and give value to your potential customer. Your goal is to get this potential customer on your email list. In saying that, there's no harm advertising a promotion and including a discount code or coupon which can be used to purchase your product or service.

RSS Feed Is Really Simple

An RSS feed is typically found on a website or blog. RSS is known as Really Simple Syndication. It is a web feed that is used to publish content in an XML format. Readers can then subscribe to your feed, and they can read fresh posts on your website or blog using an RSS Reader or Aggregator.

For all of my RSS feeds I use FeedBurner.com, which is owned by Google. FeedBurner has a very easy to use interface and provides data on the number of subscribers to your feed. FeedBurner also gives you the option for your readers to receive your feed by email.

Here's a helpful tutorial on setting up RSS feeds, by Sue Walters - here's the link http://theedublogger.com/2010/01/26/setting-up-feedburner-rss-and-email-subscription-for-your-blog/

Automated Social Media Marketing my Weapon of Choice

If you know me or have read any of my books or articles on marketing, you will be familiar with my advocacy for Social Adr. If you can afford $19 per month, I recommend Social Adr - click here to sign up for an account at www.socialadr.com. You can cancel at any time since it's a monthly subscription.

Social Adr is an automated online program which allows other users to share and post your message on their social media accounts. At this time a message can be posted on 30 high PR social media sites.

In brief Social Adr works by you creating a message with a link and the other users will then share your message across their social media accounts. You can bookmark multiple messages and your message will be fired out across the globe on autopilot.

Email List Building 'How to Use AWeber'

Email list building is a vital part of a successful online marketing strategy. Simply put, list building is a method where you capture prospects details, and then carefully build a relationship and turn these prospects into loyal customers. To encourage visitors to sign up to your list, you will offer them a free gift or newsletter.

The key is not to spam them, and the ultimate objective is to gain their trust and build relationships. From experience the best way to approach list building is to deploy a 4 to 1 formula. You need to email to your list 4 emails that only contain useful content and the 5th email should be a promotional or sales based email. If you send your list too many sales focused emails in succession, you will for sure lose the trust of the people on your list and they will unsubscribe.

Another tip is not to send your list emails on a daily or weekly basis. I therefore recommend only sending an email every 10- 14 days, in addition mixing up the frequency and leaving 30 days between some emails works well.

There are a number of free and paid for online applications to build a subscriber list. I've tried most of these subscriber online tools, and by far, my favorite is www.aweber.com because it's simple to use and has some great features. Below is a tutorial on how to set up a list using Aweber.

Go to AWeber.com and sign up for an account. In the first month they offer a $1 trial and then it costs $19 per month. $19 might seem expensive, but believe me, its great value and a nice return on investment.

Now Log in to your AWeber account and do the following:

- Click on Create and Manage List on the top of the page.

- Click Create List on the top right.

- Basic information – Complete all the fields: List Name, List Description, From, Email Address, Contact Address.

- Notifications – Add your name and email address. When someone signs up to your list, you'll receive an automatic email from AWeber letting you know that someone has signed up. Click Save.

Company Branding

Step 1 - Complete the Company Name, Website URL and Email Signature fields. For Company Name use your full name if you prefer. Then upload your logo. I prefer to upload a photo of myself to help engage with my readers.

Social Media Sharing

Step 2 - Connect with your Twitter and Facebook accounts. This is effective since your activity will be displayed on your timelines and your followers can like or share your sign up form.

Step 3 - Global Text Snippets is only useful if you want to display your shop opening times. If you don't have a retail shop ignore this part. Now click Save Settings.

Confirmed Opt-In Field

Your Confirmation Message

Step 1 - This what someone receives immediately after they sign up on your form. You can edit the Subject Line, Intro and Signature to make your message more personal.

Require Opt-In Web Forms

Step 2 - Select the On box - this will reduce the number of spammers who attempt to sign up on your form.

Success Page

Step 3 - This is the page that the subscriber sees after they have clicked and agreed to the confirmation email. If you leave this field blank, AWeber will use their standard template. Alternatively, you can create a landing page on your blog or website and the paste the landing page's URL into the field. You could also paste a link to a download of a free gift such as an eBook or Video. My preference is to leave all the URL fields blank and when the subscriber receives the first autoresponder, this email will contain the link to their free gift. All they have to do is click the link and grab their free gift.

If you sign up for my Free Twitter Guide you will see the simple email that is sent using the autoresponder which contains the link to download my free eBook.

- Now click on the Sign Up Forms on the top menu bar.
- Click Create a Sign Up Form and you will be taken to the design page for sign up forms. Here you can choose a form from the 100's of templates.

Tip: When creating a sign up form, it's proven that you will get less subscribers when you ask for too much information and personal details. So to maximize your sign up form success, just ask for their email address. If you really want their name, just ask for their first name only.

Now save your form and click Go To Step 2. On the next page you will need to create a form for your website or blog. You will also have the opportunity to supply a thank you custom URL to your blog or website. If you leave this field blank, AWeber will use their own default email which will be fine.

Next click Advanced Settings and ensure that Start On Message is set to Welcome Message (1st Follow Up). Save your form and go to Step 3 Publish.

On the Publish page, you have various options to install the form on your site. For simplicity, I always use the Javascript Snippet which is found under 'I Will Install My Form'. Highlight the Javascript and copy the code and paste it on your website or blog. The best page on your website or blog to paste the code is on a Squeeze Page. I shall cover this next since squeeze pages convert better in terms of gaining subscribers for your free gift or newsletter. Now each time you edit your form, the changes will automatically be displayed on your website or blog.

Autoresponder

Next we need to set up the message or messages the subscriber receives through the autoresponder. Click on Follow Up Series and edit and add your follow up messages. My advice is to add your free gift's download link to the 1st autoresponder email. After a few days set the 2nd autoresponder message and send a message thanking them again and asking if they enjoyed your free gift.

By doing this you will find that some of your subscribers will send you a reply email thanking you for your free gift. This is priceless as you can now start to build a relationship with this person.

When you have more than one follow up message, you will need to set the parameters on when the subscriber should receive each message. The rule of thumb with follow up messages is not to send a promotional message until every 5th message as previous mentioned. Ensure each message provides value to the subscriber before you send them a promotional message and remember not to spam them!

Broadcasts

You will also see Broadcasts on the Messages tab. Use Broadcasts when you want to send a specific email to all of your subscribers. For example, when you want to share something of value.

Tip: With every message you create, always test the message by sending it to yourself before you click Save. Another tip is not to make your message too fancy with HTML code. Keep them simple and if you can, use plain text. If you use fancy HTML and your subscriber has HTML turned off on their PC, your message will look awful and they will most likely hit the delete key.

Send Your Email Subscribers Automatic Article Updates

Whilst we are discussing Aweber, I want to share with you another great feature Aweber offers. It is the ability to send your email subscribers an automatic update when you publish an article on your Wordpress site. Aweber does this using RSS, and all you do is install their Wordpress plugin on your site and set up the Blog Broadcast on the Aweber site. You can either send the update instantly or place them in a queue for you to manually check and send. Here's a helpful link which explains more: https://help.aweber.com/hc/en-us/articles/204031076-How-Do-I-Integrate-My-Wordpress-Blog-With-AWeber-

Squeeze Page Is an Essential Page for Your Blog or Website

To capture a visitor's or prospect's email address and add them to your email list, you need to set up a squeeze page. A squeeze page is a dedicated page where a visitor lands and has 2 options – to sign up for your free gift or newsletter or to leave your website. Remember this is the page that you send your visitor to when they click your URL link – for example, the link in your free eBook.

When creating a squeeze page, you should not include any links to articles or ways for the visitor to get tempted and start looking around your site. If you look at the squeeze page on my blog you will notice there's no articles links, I only include basic pages such as Contact to make my squeeze look more authentic.

Generally a squeeze page should include a bold headline, sub headline, bullet points to highlight the content, an image, a sign up form and some form of call to action. Another point about squeeze pages is you should track them to see the percentage of your visitors who actually follow through and sign up. If you are using Wordpress I recommend the Pretty Link plugin.

Pretty Link allows you to create a unique URL for any website page and will display the number of times this unique link has been clicked. By knowing the number of clicks and number of downloads during a certain time frame, you can then track and work out the percentage of sign ups. By knowing the percentages you can then make subtle changes to your squeeze page and see if more people sign up for your free gift.

Write an Ebook and Give It Away as a Free Gift

I'm now going to let you know an awesome strategy to get subscribers on your email list. It involves creating a free eBook that contains unique content your prospects will find valuable. I have used this strategy and it can produce excellent results. What we are going to do is create two eBooks and use both of them to spread the word about your product or service and get more subscribers on your email list. I must confess this strategy works best if your product or service is global or as a minimum, country based. It will not work very well if you cover a local area with your product or service.

Initially you need to create two eBooks that are related to your product or service, each book will be approximately 5-7,000 words. You need to write the book so the reader can see you're an authority and expert in your business niche. When you have completed your books, one will be your free gift for your email list and the other will be published on Amazon and www.Smashwords.com.

This book will contain the link to your free gift or squeeze page – Smashwords will distribute your book to other online book stores such as Barnes & Noble, Apple iBooks, Sony etc. This book will be priced at $0.00; yes it will be a free book. When you have a free eBook published on all these book sites, you could expect over 100 people per day to download your book. What this means is that potential customers will sign up for your free gift and you then have their email address to follow up with your autoresponder.

The other benefit is that over 100 people per day will be introduced to your product, service or company. If you only manage to engage with 1 or 2 of these people, over a course of the year this could be an extra 350-700 customers. Now imagine if you published multiple free eBooks – can see you see why this is an awesome strategy.

How to Starting Writing Your New Book

Open your mind and flood the paper - forget about grammar!

If you're like me, your head at this stage should be flooded with ideas for your new book and you can't wait to start writing. My guess is this is simply human nature! Grab your A4 pad and in a quiet environment with no distractions, let's flood the paper with all the ideas flowing around in your brain.

Do not worry or focus on grammar or the correct spellings, we are simply extracting the words and phrases from our heads. Keep it unique and write down as many words and phrases as possible. Consult any notes that you previous made and jot them down. Many authors say they prefer to write in a coffee shop since there are no distractions. Lucky for me I have a home office, so when the kids are at school or in bed, I lock myself away when writing. Next we shall discuss building the outline structure.

The Framework to Build Upon - The Outline

First off, we need to create the structure and add the words to the structure from your A4 pad. I always like to create 5 main headings and then create 3-5 sub headings under each main heading - so in total 15-25 headings for my words. So go through your words and any ideas you have create 5 headings with the subheadings.

Don't be too strict at this stage, all you need to do is list all your words and phrases under a relevant heading. Again do not get hung up on grammar or spellings. You notice that I mention using an A4 pad, to be honest using paper or your word processor software is fine. I prefer paper and pen since my typing skills are not that quick.

As you complete the subheadings by adding your words, cross out the words on your writing pad. Complete each subheading so when finished all the words on your writing pad are crossed out. Now you should have plenty of words listed under the subheadings to begin writing paragraphs and using these words as prompts.

If you do choose to use a word processor application like MS Word, sign up for a free account at Dropbox.com and this way you can backup your work using the cloud.

Publishing Your Free Ebook

At the time of writing this book, Amazon has the largest marketplace for eBooks and is the market leader. The problem with Amazon is that you cannot publish a free book. If you sign up to their KDP Select program, you can advertise your book for free for 5 days during each 90 day period.

When you sign up for KDP Select, you are not permitted to publish your book on other sites such as Smashwords, iBooks etc. For this eBook strategy to work and you get the most from it, you need your book published on Amazon for free.

Now the good news is there's a way to get your book published on Amazon for free. To do this, you need to publish your eBook on Smashwords and then add it to their Premium Catalog - the Premium Catalog is a service where Smashwords distribute a book to the following online book stores:

Premium Catalog, automatically distributes it to major online retailers such as Apple (distribution to iBookstores in 51 countries), Barnes & Noble (US and UK), Sony, Kobo, Flipkart, Diesel eBook Store, eBooks Eros (operated by Diesel), Baker & Taylor (Blio and the Axis360 library service), Page Foundry (operates retail sites Inktera.com and Versent.com; and operates Android ebook store apps for Cricket Wireless and Asus). Additionally, Kobo powers the ebook stores of multiple ebook retailers around the world.

Simply by distributing to Kobo via Smashwords, your books will also reach WH Smith in the UK, FNAC in France and Portugal, Livraria

Cultura in Brazil, Angus & Robertson in Australia, Bookworld in Australia, Indigo in Canada, Collins in Australia, Feltrinelli in Italy, Libris in the Netherlands, Paper Plus in New Zealand, Play in Great Britain, Rakuten in Japan, Buy.com (now Rakuten) in the US, Whitcoulls in New Zealand.

Here's a link to help you publish an eBook on Smashwords, this should get you started. http://www.smashwords.com/about/how_to_publish_on_smashwords

All these eBook stores allow you to advertise your book for free. Now to get your book accepted by Smashwords, you need to format it a special way so that it complies with the e-pub standard. For $5 go to www.fiverr.com and buy a Smashwords Formatting gig. All you need to do is upload your MS Word eBook and let the Fiverr seller format your book. Smashwords can take a few weeks before your book is accepted and distributed to the other eBook stores. When you add your book to the Smashword Premium Catalog, I advise you to check your Smashword dashboard daily incase they reject your book's formatting.

Publishing Your eBook Free on Amazon – This Is How

You can publish your eBook on Amazon Kindle either before or after you publish on Smashwords – the choice is yours. It's very simple to publish your book on Amazon Kindle, visit https://kdp.amazon.com and sign up for a free self publishing account. Visit this link if you need to find out more about KDP Publishing, these FAQ's should help you. https://kdp.amazon.com/self-publishing/help?topicId=A36BYK5S7AJ2NQ.

Now wait until your eBook has been accepted and distributed to all the Smashwords Premium Catalog of book stores and your eBook has been published on Amazon. Amazon's policy is to price match books, so if the same book is cheaper on another bookstore, they will match the price.

You now need to find your book on the other bookstores such as iBooks, Smashwords, Barnes and Noble and copy your eBook's URL on these sites. Now ask a few friends and family to click on the 'tell us about a lower price?' which is found under your book's sales rank on Amazon.

Your friends and family need to click this link and complete the form. They will need to paste your books URL found on the other bookstores. Make sure they state they saw your book advertised for free. Now you need to wait as Amazon do drag their feet, it might take a few weeks before you see your book advertised for free.

" Did we miss any relevant features for this product? Tell us what we missed.

Would you like to give feedback on images or tell us about a lower price? "

Now that you have your book published on Amazon, I recommend you set up an author account at https://authorcentral.amazon.com. Some authors are not aware of the benefits you receive by utilizing Amazon Author Central. In the next section I will cover Amazon Author Central in more detail and hopefully it will give you an idea how use it to gain the most benefit.

Amazon Author Central You Need Use It for Maximum Effect

Amazon's Author Central is an extra tool at your fingertips to help you promote books.

At this time you need a separate Author Central account for the following countries: United States, United Kingdom, France, Germany, and Japan. To start with, sign up for an Author Central account using the United States link. If you have an Amazon account, then you can use this to sign up. Here's the US link to https://authorcentral.amazon.com/

Add Your Books

Click on the Books tab, which is at the top, and add your books while using the search box. A great feature of Author Central is that it allows you to use a pen name if you've used one with your books. When you add your book, click the link to let Amazon know you are the author. Your pen name will be added after you agree the confirmation email. Now you can switch author names in a dropdown menu, which is found on the top right of the page.

Here's a tip: Some of the categories on Amazon are not listed in your self-publishing account. If you want to change the category for your book, copy and paste the category and send Amazon an email by clicking Contact Us.

Profile

Next, complete your profile by clicking on the Profile tab in the top menu bar. Complete your bio with a minimum of 100 characters. Add your Facebook URL and Twitter URL. Now upload your photo.

Blog Feed

If you have a blog, add your RSS feed URL by clicking Add Blog. Personally, I think the easiest way to display your blog posting is to sign up for a FeedBurner.com account and add the URL they create and give you. Typically, your blog postings will show up within a 24 hour period.

Twitter

Add your Twitter username, for example, @username. This will display your Twitter feed.

Videos

If you have any stored videos, then why not upload them to promote your author brand.

Books Tab

After you've uploaded your books you can then click on your book, which is listed when you click on Books. Now you have three tabs: Editorial Reviews, Book Details, and Book Extras. Under Editorial Reviews, one of the options is to edit Product Description. Once you edit your book's description in Author Central, you will not be able to make amendments of your description using your KDP Publisher's account. Under Editorial Reviews, you can add reviews that you obtained elsewhere. To do this, click the Edit button next to Review.

How to Create a Profitable Email Sales Funnel

So what is an email sales funnel you might ask? Well, great question so let me explain. An email sales funnel is a process that takes a prospect on a journey to becoming a buyer. The journey starts when the prospect visits a landing page and exchanges their email address for a free product. During this journey the seller gains the trust of the prospect by sharing free useful tips – these useful tips could be in the form of a video, article or ebook. The idea is for you to become a thought leader in the prospect eyes and then close them with a sales focused email to sell your money product. A typical email sales funnel could be three, four or more emails which are sent daily. All emails will be automated and sent by an email marketing platform such as Aweber, GetResponse, Mailchimp etc. Each email will be sent using an autoresponder. An autoresponder is a tool which allows you to schedule an email to be sent at a certain time following a person signing up to an email list.

Here's an email sales funnel structure I use:

Day 1: Create a landing page offering a free product in exchange for the prospects email address. Immediately send the prospect a follow up email with the link to download your free product.

Day 2: Send the prospect an email asking if they enjoyed your free product and subtly introduce your money product. Do not sell your money product at this stage. It's good practice to include a video of you in this email to build trust.

Day 3: Send the prospect an email introducing another of your free products or useful article or video. Again subtly include a link or an image of your money product.

Day 4: Send the prospect a sales email. Go for the close, sell them your money product and tell them why they should buy it and how it will solve their pain. My advice here is to sell them a low cost product between $5 and $30. At this stage of the funnel, the prospect should be warm and will hopefully trust you. If the prospect buys your product, you need to get them off your prospect email list and move them over to a customer list. To do this the prospect will need to complete a form which can be integrated with the shopping cart. If you use Aweber or GetResponse, you will be able to set up automated rules to unsubscribe them from the prospect list and move them to a customer list. Once they are on your customer list you can spend time engaging and building more trust with them and sell these customers more products.

The great thing about automated rules is that if the prospect does not buy at this stage, you could email them a few more times and try to get them to buy your product. Then when they do buy, they will automatically be added to a customer list. I use an online platform called JVZoo.com to sell my products. JVZoo integrates with Aweber and GetResponse which makes it seamless when a prospect becomes a customer and moved to a customer list. The move from one list to another happens on the checkout page when using JVZoo. Although I prefer Aweber, JVZoo (in my opinion) does work better with GetResponse because JVZoo owns GetResponse.

Redirect a Domain Name Bluehost Web Hosting

If you have seen any of my online articles, presentations, etc., you would have noticed http://www.ebooksbydarren.com/. This redirects to my Amazon Author Central account. The reason I have created a redirect is that it looks more professional than my Author Central URL.

When would you use a redirect domain name? Good question let me give you an example. Let's say that one of your competitors goes bust (for whatever reason), and their website or domain name is well known and receives a large number of daily visitors. You could purchase your competitors domain name and redirect it to your website. So, when someone clicks your competitor's domain name, the visitor will be redirected to your website.

Another cheeky way to use redirects is taking advantage of misspelled words. A user might mis-type a URL – let's use the domain name 'example.com' and pretend they are a competitor. A user might type "exmple.com" and "exmaple.com". If you bought these 2 misspelled domain names, you could redirect them to your website and receive extra visitors to your website.

I have been using Bluehost for many years. For a small annual fee around $80, you can host unlimited websites or blogs and easily create redirect domains and build WordPress sites. Furthermore, you can easily transfer your websites and your email addresses to Bluehost. If you need any help give them a call since they are very helpful.

Here's how to set up a redirect using cPanel found at Bluehost.com:

- Sign up for an account at www.bluehost.com.

- Once you have signed up for an account, click Control Panel Login.

- Now enter your login details and sign in.

- You should now see the cPanel. On the cPanel you can perform multiple tasks, including creating email addresses, installing WordPress and much, much more.

- Scroll down to the Domain Management and click Register Domain.

- Now search Choose and Purchase Your Domain. If you can, always try and purchase a .com domain.

- Go back to cPanel. Click on Domain Management, then click Domain Manager.

- Now you will see your domain name listed, and it will be marked Unassigned.

- Click Unassigned and you will see the Assign Domain page.
Make sure the following are selected:

- Enter Domain: Use a domain that is already associated with your account.

- Choose Addon vs Parked: Addon domain.

- Choose Addon Directory and Sub-domain: Create a new directory.

- Now click Assign This Domain.

- Whilst in Domain Management, you should see Redirect in the top menu bar. Click on the Redirect URL.

- Under Add Redirect, ensure Permanent (301) is selected.

- Directly underneath you will see http://(www.)?. Use the dropdown and select your domain name. Mine would be DarrenAckers.com.

- Then, in the box under Redirects, enter your destination domain name.

- Then ensure Redirect with or without WWW is selected.

- Finally, click Add this Redirect.

And that's it! Congratulations! This is how you create a permanent Redirect.

More Cool Apps and Tools

How to Track and Learn an Email Has Been Opened

HubSpot Sidekick is an email tracking tool which lets you know when someone has opened and read your email. To use Sidekick, you must first add the app to your Google Chrome browser and install it on your Outlook email program. The tracking works by adding a small HTML pixel to your email which sends a signal to you when the email is opened. Unfortunately if the receiver of your email had images turned off in Outlook or viewed your email in plain text, the pixel would not fire and you would not learn if your email had been opened. This applies to most tracking applications. Let's be honest, the minority of folk do not know how to switch off images downloading in Outlook.

A Cool Screen Capture Tool

I would like to introduce you to a free screen capture application called ScreenShooter. I love this tool! ScreenShooter lets you share instantly what you see on your desktop. You press 'F9" on your keyboard, select an area of the desktop which you would like to copy and either copy the image, save the image or share the image with a unique URL.

Conclusion

I would like to say thank you for choosing my book since there are a large number of similar Kindle books. Would you be so kind to tell your friends, family and work colleagues about my book?

After all, you should be able to easily make 1000 times the $3 that you spent on this book. Positive feedback directly affects other readers' reviews and leads to additional orders.

Please can you write a review about this book on Amazon?

If you would like to connect, please do so using the following and let me know you bought my book:

Blog http://www.darrenackers.com/
Twitter https://twitter.com/darren_ackers
LinkedIn https://uk.linkedin.com/in/darrenackers

In addition, if you need any help, advice, or feel I missed something in this book, please do email me admin@darrenackers.com - I would love to hear from you.

The very best of luck

Darren